PRAISE FOR *BLOODFRESH*

"*BloodFresh* by Ebony Stewart is a stunning collection of robust poems. This assembly of work gives the reader a glimpse into the details of the author's life while allowing the audience an opportunity to find pieces of themselves within the narratives. Ebony finds brilliant and lucid ways of discussing heavy topics and pairs them with beautiful moments of self-discovery. This book is about survival, celebration, and everything in between.

—RUDY FRANCISCO, AUTHOR OF *I'LL FLY AWAY*

"Ebony Stewart's *BloodFresh* speaks to what Zakiyyah Iman Jackson theorizes about the demand for Black(ened) people to be subhuman, human, and superhuman at the same time. Stewart reminds us that this is true especially for Black queer women. In BloodFresh, Stewart negotiates the costs of these demands made on the labor, time, bodies, etc. of Black women who, according to Nanny in Zora Neale Hurston's *Their Eyes Were Watching God*, are 'de mule[s] uh de world.' And so, *BloodFresh* is a reckoning. It is a book that will read you, dear reader. Stewart is incisive—"I choose violence," she says in the poem 'Pockets'—and believe me, *BloodFresh* is a knife. If it cuts—*and yes it does!*—it is only to get to the heart of what ails us. In that way, it is healing. Especially for those 'born in babylon / both nonwhite and woman' as Lucille Clifton puts it, it is a mentor text on what it looks like to shape 'a kind of life' when you don't have any models. It is a prayer *and* a spell. Prophetic and punk AF, this here is a collection and poet you won't forget anytime soon. As Stewart herself announces in the poem that begins the collection, "My name is Ebony. / I promise you won't forget. / I am half demigoddess and beast."

—AYOKUNLE FALOMO, AUTHOR OF *AFRICANAMERICAN'T*

"*BloodFresh* is about Reclaiming so much of what we've all lost. This book gives us our joy back and allows us decide who to share that newly reclaimed joy with. *BloodFresh* is Brilliant, it's necessary, it's family, it's everything we were searching for home again."

—NATASHA T. MILLER, AUTHOR OF BUTCHER

"This collection of poems, mantras and mandates provides Stewart's forthright stance on "telling it like it is", powered by a heartfelt intensity and ideology from her own experiences as a Black Queer Woman and working professional from the south. *BloodFresh* gives us a glimpse of how her many intersections are bursting at the seams and all she requests is Pockets in return for her labor.

The closing piece, *Mental Health_Barz*, a piece I have taught SO many times, carries us forward into a conversation around gaslighting and invalidating the very human moments of strong public figures. BloodFresh is relevant, gripping, and unrelenting in its demand of keeping the light."

—ROYA MARSH, AUTHOR OF DAYLIGHT

"Ebony Stewart is a revolutionary poet and her work is so necessary for this moment. Her words are electrically inspiring for those who wish to engage more deeply with our society. Ebony's unmistakable poetic voice explores what it has always meant to be Black, to be a woman, to be vulnerable, empowered and yet to be human. Her art gives us the language to articulate the subtleties and complexities of life. *BloodFresh* is a fluid blend of pain, joy, culture, and nuance. You owe it to yourself to read this book."

—ANGELA T. RYE, POLITICS AND CULTURE COMMENTATOR

BLOODFRESH

BLOODFRESH

Poems By

Ebony Stewart

Button Publishing Inc.

Minneapolis

2022

◇

Published by Button Poetry / Exploding Pinecone Press
Minneapolis, MN 55403 | http://www.buttonpoetry.com

◇

All Rights Reserved
Manufactured in the United States of America
Edited by: Michael Whalen
Cover design: Nikki Clark
Cover artist: Dogon Krigga
www.artbykrigga.com
ISBN 978-1-63834-008-9
26 25 24 23 22   1 2 3 4 5

FOR THE ENGLISH PROFESSOR & OTHERS WHO CAN'T RELATE TO MY WORK & COULDN'T SNATCH THE DREAM FROM ME:

For the fights in middle school, in high school, in undergrad, and as a graduate student. These hands still work. This mind still sharp. I hope it cuts. But don't die yet. Not until you see me make it look BloodFresh to death.

For the stories I've never told. Speak of secrets I'll never tell. I am everywhere. I see everything. I remember. I save all my receipts. My phone run slow. This mouth too quick. They know I know. Petty like God. Made in God's image. You feel me? Yeah, you do.

For the time my ex called the police. Men who return love with fear and control, call me his & then drag me. For the unhealthy men in my life & the ones I wish I never had or knew. Your life changed because of me; your life you'll never be able to live the same without me. You didn't kill me, so I still won.

For the ones who cuss & don't know from hard. I learned all my dangerous by watching you. *Wow*. Behold the original savages. For the women. The not yet. For the undo. They can't tell. You did for you what you needed to be done.

For the dope ones, the dealers, & children home alone raising themselves to rise. What up, blood? What's crackin', cuh? Stay alive, homie. Just. Stay alive.

For the loss & missing & never to return. Wherever you are. Wherever you go. Welcome home.

I had a sister once. When I see her, I might cry, yell, & scream. Our mother's 1st born. I love you. I love you. I love you. Our father's favorite. It hurts every time I have to remind myself to let go. For the ones who have to let go. There's water & then there's blood. The body needs both. I'll see you at the funeral.

For the ones who never get the love they know they deserve. I hope you have a safety plan. It's never too late to be a good person.

For the Sun, the Moon, and those of us who be both.

For those who still read books.
Hoarders, if you can hear me,
I love you, too.

For the ones who ask what's next:
Are you not entertained or are you just never satisfied? If you celebrated people properly, you wouldn't keep needing more.

For when it's not a poem,
It's a prayer or a clap-back
or whatever I forgot to say before I went silen(t)(c)ed or however I act when I'm hungry.

I wanna apologize,
but I'm not really sorry.[1]

---

1. after Kevin Gates' "Really Really"

BEASTS

Poets
were once born in Babylon with yellow and purple bruises
for scarlet seals not meant for pain but translated to holy.
We wrote Psalms and I Corinthians, and then an angel with green
wings sold us to King James. Now, we speak in Revelations.
Our words
were stolen from our throats, so now we converse in Hell.
My people have been divided.
The chosen legacy of ancient survivors
who vowed to carry out their purpose
are now known as *Beasts*.
We bleed the ink of whatever poem last written
as keepsakes for our dying mere mortals,
laborers of timeless themes baring our souls from generation
to generation.
We are Beasts
sent to defend and revive language.
We are the stirring tale of a hero growing into poets
long overdue—awaiting our reward.
We are the saviors of the universe destroying thy enemies.
They called us aliens once,
because we have recoiled tongues that spit like javelins.
My kind are not to be confused.
We are godlike in Bible terms, meaning, make them love you
and fear you on the same page.
By our exhale, we shove the penises and nipples of those defeated
down their nostrils, so they can smell their own filth.
We do not come in peace.
We see what you do with it.
"War on the flesh, famine unto death, greed for salvation."
Peace,
      we see what you do with it.
As if it's not enough you've contaminated my people's minds
to make them sell out on darkness and confuse good with light,

you've raped a race of poetic spirits, so they have no choice
but to reject their bodies.
A man was lynched yesterday.
And we are not allowed to weep at the world . . .
we'll be too busy
removing bullet fragments from our tongues.
And your government is corrupt.
I no longer ask what my country can do for me
or what I can do for my country.
No.
Tonight, time meets fate.
My name is Ebony.
I promise you won't forget.
I am half demigoddess and beast.
A female warrior, dexterity over the male breed, highly sought after.
Carnal and infectious.
Calming a confrontational language by the threat of my words
crushing into their veins like velvet.
Mixed with black widow in my pen;
inked.
And they have no choice but to become unraveled.
A deity.
Poets come to my palette for fellowship and sleep.
No matter the blasphemous virtuosity under their nails
and creativity impregnated in their bellies.
Silence begins the mouth when the brain stops thinking.
So, ignite at the pluck of my voice.
I am the electric guitar cotton fields needed.
Maybe then our origin would be of anarchy.

> Your rights have been taken.
> Don't you want them back?

Poets,
move through space—walk as if poems
have become your shadow.
Break the patterns,
write on shredded paper,
do not become complacent in the holocaust

ciphered in our midst.
Keep your poems for memories—this, they cannot take.
Be the voice, the verse, and the narrative.
For this moment may never come again.
And she quotes, "There is no greater agony than bearing
an untold story."[2]

Beasts,
continue to be a prism of sunlight,
so when the pages fall like midnight,
we will be ready
to open up our mouths
and fight.

2. Maya Angelou's "I Know Why the Caged Bird Sings"

CONTENTS

Blood, as in lineage, as in fresh ink, fresh blood, fresh to death, countertransference, relation, fluid, oxygen, existing, changing, being, beating, a body and its forgiveness, the plague, bleeding, anew, birth, spilling, open, what is love, completely consumed.

BLOODFRESH

I.

I DON'T HAVE A FALLBACK PLAN, BECAUSE I DON'T PLAN TO FALL BACK.

TRANSPARENT

I always have a hard time writing about myself.
It's easier to tell someone else's story.
And I'm still trying to convince my shadow
that it chose me for a reason.

When I was a little girl, my first word was "NO."
I bit people and stopped eating and talking at 10 p.m.
I grew breasts before I knew what to do with them.
See, I knew
there would be so many times I'd want to say yes and mean it.
Biting gave me a head start at getting back at people. And since I
asked so many questions by 10 o'clock, I was exhausted.
My breasts reminded me I was a second-class citizen
in a world of d*cks.
Every time Johnny Hart would pull my bra strap, I wished breasts
came with receipts.
Being a young woman is so hard.

I'm the youngest of three, so people naturally love me.
I'm awkward at accepting compliments.
I get all embarrassed and *uh-uh-uh* in my head
and the only response I can come up with is "thank you" or
"thank you so much."
               Translation: I'm still learning how to love myself.
I've had the same best friend since I started liking people.
One time when I was 12, I ate a whole gallon of ice cream,
and my mom had to straw-feed me Sprite and pat my back
until I burped.
My mother can fix anything.
Her dimples are where Gods go to learn agape.
I've downgraded to popcorn.
The first boy I ever loved close enough to forever broke my heart.
My favorite color used to be pink until the same boy who was
"quicker than my innocence" separated the purest parts I had left.

So, now I don't do favorites,
but every person who gets me deep turns red.
I've been told I'm an amazing kisser, and on a platonic level,
I give really good hugs. I use all of my muscles during contact
because I never know when I'll be touched again.
And the OCD doesn't help.
Always checking and rechecking. Counting on fingers,
in my head, with my lips.
Right now, we are on number 364 of this poem . . . and counting.
I have a stitched spine with a book of poems keeping me upright.

There was a time when my parents held hands and were beautiful
together for no other reason than to be the color black.
I've never met those people.
I was the last thing they loved collectively.
I know a father who loves music and a mother who cried
like a whisper because her lover started treating her
like the base and the snare drum.
When people ask why I love the way I do, I say,
"I don't know nothing, but the 808."

I speak in clouds and concrete.
Southern-bred, Jamaican-tongued with a round
of bullets in my throat ready to go
BUK BUK BUK!
The same little girl who goes blind when she gets angry,
blacks out, and is a destroyer of all things.
My arms be like family and the first thing that ever loved you back.
And I know it sounds like I'm bipolar, but I'm not.
Okay, maybe a little bit.
It's to be expected when you have Heaven and Hell in your veins.
I speak in thunder and lightning,
bring brass knuckles and fist fights.
I knew heart when she met pain.
A jungle on my tonsils.
That same little girl who ran out of paper and started writing on walls.
When the night collapsed into my chest,
poetry saved my life.

I used to think I could turn people into things
just by squinting my eyes.
Now, I just use my words and my side-eye.
I'm still learning how to love people for who they are,
because I know being transparent isn't easy.
Trust me, I know.

MY MOTHER'S ACCENT comes out when she's angry. Curves the tongue around the throat. Sucks words from the teeth wishing a ___ would. A girl from the South. You got the right one from the hood.

YOUNG, GIFTED, & BLACK

My name is not convenient;
it is the child forgotten—
stolen from historical value.
My name is the guilt you try
to shame me with, a burden
to the grief that haunts you.
Before my name could be full
and brave, it was lynched
and barbeque skeptical.
My name has been raped,
branded, and whipped.
My name is the chocolate-milk
titty your babies clung to and from,
a forgotten protagonist of forgotten facts.

Or did you forget how the story goes?

My name is how easy it is to
misplace the truth, to strip me
of all this mighty so I can be
a life under servitude.
My name is a reminder of nigger
children who get murdered
in the South, North, East, and West.
Because my name is a threat;
my name is the absence in your amen.

Or did you forget how the stories go?

My name ain't neva got a pass—
can't. Got too much oil slick, too much
scratch, punch, and fight.
My name is real confrontational.
Ain't interested in your comfortable.

My name bite too hard.
Must've been caged.
Must've been animalistic once.
My name is only necessary after it benefits you.
You say my name ain't right.

Well, mama say everything
that has a beginning began in me,
say imma blistering queen,
say my name is a filter and
all the light gotta pass through me.
My name is a G I A N T, is rise, is healing,
is learning how to remember itself,
is the Congo—the beatin' sound you dance to.
My name is the utterance of struggle
meets pride meets grace meets visible.

Yeah, you see me reinventing myself,
reclaiming my power.
My name be the hero that freed us,
is reborn negro and new growth.
My name done trying to figure out
why you don't love me.
My name is a wealthy affirmation.
My name is what blackness done
been through and can be.
My name say I can't be impossible
because my name be in existence.

THIS POEM IS ABOUT JOY

This poem is about joy.

It's not about water
remnants evaporation or sand

or thirst or dry
fruit or hinges or

being hung   today no
one died on the

street on the side
walk in the hands

of a police officer
or guard

today a little boy
is able to play

outside and be a child
with a full imagination

today the only time
he was asked to

put his hands up
was to show us

how he looks when
he pretends he's flying

today a Black woman
could smoke a cigarette

could laugh could do
whatever in the hell she

wanted to do with
her hair

no one called me
a nigger   today blatantly

or indirectly   today they
remembered my name   today

it sounded like joy
no matter who said
it

today being Black was
not a reason to

die by its natural
causes

what I mean is
no one tried to

kill me today   no
one black or dark

skin or the wrong
shade died today

today the only time
we came inside was

to gather and tell
stories   remember

when everyday was a
funeral a sad song

and a eulogy   *oh*
but today

the only time we
cried was when we

rejoiced   the only
hashtag we used today

was #joy   today the
handkerchiefs only wanted

to feel the faces
of the ones who

cried with joy

This poem is about joy.

It's not about fear
or anger or sadness

them emotions come to
us too easy this

poem is not about
glass or porcelain or

fragile things or being
weak or tried or

broken or how many
times or how long

we gotta work for
it

This poem is about joy.

How long it stayed
how we remember it

in us
always

SO WHATCHU SAYIN'?

I know poetry.

I know 8-year-old me and me-now
still hold the pen funny I've always
had a hard time letting things go Got
a grip and an escape plan to get free But
before I let go let me get my hair braided
I know how to keep my head still bob on
beat even when everything feels off Still I
put on for my city cause we all we got In
my hood I know MLK Garth Rd and Main St run from
the east side to the south side 'til I die I betta know how
to code switch

When the gunshots pop call 'em fireworks
When the cops stop you make sure you say
yes'sa no'sa Celebrate staying alive by speaking in
compromise and concern for the oppressor I know my
momma pray in tongues and slam poetry And the point is
she wrote a check to get me outta the hood
to send me off to privilege And the whole hood'll be
there if I ever wanna go back Cause the swamp slab
slow in candy painted red and gold grills say I got
potential

but didn't know (B)lack Excellence could turn a new trick
into imposter syndrome While thinking in complex: I
know dark-skin (b)lack girls standout stand-strong and
don't get to identify as soft or delicate Forget *a Black girl
song* Women I know our value is measured by how much
we overextend While attempting to interrupt: be first
Jab. Jab. Bodywork. Bodywork. Left hook. Bob and
weave And I know I'm strong—

it's in the foot work Still I wanna be cared for And even when everything I'm tryna balance feels heavy I know how to keep my head up let the tears bob down somebody else's face "Your poems are so relatable" But did you know they don't do enough At least that's what the rejection letters say

Uh-huh Yeah Yeah Wade in the water muck and mire

The Sun'll come out tomorrow But ain't no sunshine when she's gone . . .

So whatchu sayin'?
I know flow pace and technique
I went to school for this Paid close attention to the lessons and readings teaching hate and erased me I know my professors add weight just by talking at me like I'm dumb And if you gone write about where you come from just make sure you use your inside voice Make sure it's fascinating and oppressive Rich but rags
to riches rich Rich Homie Quan (B)lack back
bending Black

make you feel some type a way or you could just retire Black phrases faces and spaces Ball 'til you fall talmbout how hard it is but not in a way that'll make white folks feel bad about what they did continue to do Is it systemic or systematic I know 8-year-old me and me-now still think in ghetto dreams & habits we did it while being poor I know white folks using the word ghetto to describe anything is a racial slur I don't care I don't care
They don't care

Cause you ain't gone write nothing worth keeping a nobody like you alive nowhere Wait Are you a writer or is your poetry not white conforming enough A (B)lack person was murdered today   should I write it in a way that makes you forget how much it hurts or distracts from

the pain Everything I do I did while bleeding blood and
constructing a breathtaking poem on pages
Added the word nigga just so white folks can feel what
it's like to have their tongues in cages

I know I have no interest in writing poetry born of
suffrage and sacrifice Still I gotta make use of strong
literary devices to elevate how divisive it feels to be
divided from how I feel about existing While being me: I
know some Black literaries gatekeeping white spaces
Wanna be in spaces that don't wanna make space for all
of us A new case of gentrification I know what it's like to
entrust and be tricked by a favorite unable to keep their
promises Abusers can literally write anything
including activism as performance I know what it's like
to mourn a hero that became an overseer to the hood's
trauma And you can't say Gotta keep harmful idols alive
and understood It's so unstable I had to unbraid my truth
from the table
This crown be weighted Blood Still have a hard time
letting things go Temporarily blinded Saul Paul me a
poet but keep quiet And silence be the language of
Gawds

This, I know.

AFFIRMATION #_____

Your name is in rooms your feet haven't entered yet.
Your name is in the mouths of folks you don't know,
but they rock wit you.
Your name is a Gawd and you are worthy of these praises.
Your name brings good fortune.
Bless the body it belongs to.

GAWD OF GAPS

So, I go to the dentist for a teeth cleaning
and the dentist keep asking me about braces
I ain't missing no teeth, but this gap be wild!
I got one mouth and a gap that greet you when
I smile or say f*ck you   My daddy gave me
this gap, so you gotta know I mean it
You gotta know this gap how my mama know I'm his,
so I gotta keep it   Still empress to this fallen empire
I suck my teeth with disdain A dental habit I ain't willing to change
My gap speak Afro-Caribbean, pursed lips, and a country ass   b*tch please
My mouth clean, it's these gaps that cuss
How everything I'm thinking get free
Cause all my thoughts be   from outer space
This here   be my mound of Venus
I part my lips and I'm   infinity and beyond
Separate from anything and still a physical feeling
I pray to the Gawd of Gaps   that a gap be wide enough to
make you and all 100 billion galaxies jealous   My teeth be overzealous
get the glory to any joke you make
Cause my gap expanded   and got the last laugh anyway
You can't close the light out of dis here mouth,   ever
Sometimes I sound like gravel,
sometimes I sound like coffee and cream[3]
But every time my gap speak,   it say what it mean
          My gap be a landscape
I brought the cool air & wealth of my country with me
We and the teeth say,   f*****ck   yo standard of beauty
          We be a good thing that lasted
Mirror, mirror, on the wall,   some of my words gotta lisp when they talk
But that don't mean I'm starving the proper way of speaking
My gap just whistle while it work   Say   gimme   my   space
We just look like this trust me we're loved
Even if you got   an acquired taste

---

3. Nina Simone

BURNT SUGAR

My mom tells the story of one of the first times she took me outside as a baby, she brought me to the church house. Folks crowded around with big eyes to see the child they said resembled a baby doll. Chocolate. Ebony skin. "Hair like silk," they said. My mother gleamed holding her Black child natural and pure sweet. An organic offering from the Creator. And Ms. Brown came over, peeked in paper-bag tested, and said, "This baby *is* what they say she *is*— beautiful—but, I'm sorry . . . I'm just partial to light-skin babies."

Blacktose intolerant.

Just like racism. Equally as violent. Also known as *colorism*. A prejudice or discrimination against individuals with a darker skin tone, typically among people of the same ethnic or racial group given to them by European colonizer standards, with a slave mentality, that looks down on others, and has an infinity for whiteness. See me and immediately try to shrink my spirit. And I grow to question but harden this exterior. An outer layer marks me as undesirable. Even though there are 64 different variations and distinctions of brown skin Black people all over the world, lighter skin and ethnicity ain't never spared none of us.

But it be your own people.

My dark-skin cousin with a dark-skin mama & grandmama told me, "Every Black man want a redbone, light-skin, badass yella bone." And all I can hear is how low his self-esteem is. How bad he wanna be a white man. Black men have always wanted something better than where they come from, even if it's their women. "And if she dark-skin, she gotta have a good body." Cause why else would anybody want me unless my body is desirable enough to prefer? I am reminded of how much harder I have to love the self-hate anyone Black is running from while healing the wounds of those with a darker hue. I ask internalized racism passed down and perpetuated by the media: is she pretty or is she light-skin?

Am I dark-skin or are you unable to let me forget it? Do I ever get to just be pretty without a dejected rhetoric or a backhanded compliment? Is the complexion of my skin the reason why light-skin keeps getting lighter and lighter? Is the photographer a good photographer if they don't know how to work with color? Are dark-skin Black women less likely to be married because colorism can't picture it? Does a tattoo artist really have talent if they've only ever tatted light-skin girls with a dark side? Is this why dark-skin women reside in prison with longer sentences? Is darkness only ever thought of as sinister? Or is my villain origin story placed in an idea that I should still have to save a world that excludes or refuses to choose me? Do I remind them of everything, especially the physiological deterioration based in "not white" healing?

I am not a new thing. Grown now, if I could, I would ask Ms. Brown to stop doing the work of whiteness. I'd snap my so Black they're magic fingers to get her and them unstuck from being colorstruck. Un-underestimate me. Unhate me. See me and love me better than that which you've subscribed to. Vamoose and undo colorist thoughts and attitudes. This pan-racial community color palette I belong to. Lay down your burdened language anywhere that doesn't keep conflict or make difference. I wanna trace back our roots and unsuffer its unspoken shame. I wanna derail, offset, and unsail the slave trade's trauma voyage. I wanna be respected, admired, and cared for with the same fervor you do white women.

I wanna be a Black girl, entirely, whose worth is not measured in the anguish of being dark-skin.

808S & HEARTBREAK

I love my mama like Kanye love his

The doctor says it's congestive heart failure, but
not like what we think Heart failure does not mean the heart stops
working Instead, the heart works less efficiently from being
overworked

A little thing that turns into a big thing A silly argument in a marriage
that leads to divorce You think you have a cold—turns out, it's really
the flu One time, I drove with my check engine light on for an entire
month

because I had sh*t to do
because I didn't have the money
because who else gone get it done
When I finally had time to take my car in,

the mechanic said if ida went one more day
the engine would've gave way/stopped working/burnt out
To compensate, the heart might stretch, pump harder, or try to give
more And I've never known a more accurate way

to describe Black women How fitting a condition for us Always the
one we been waiting for, but they need And the riddle reads:
>What is so strong, but isn't allowed to be weak   or
>Whose heart has it harder, but still

goes harder until their heart hardens or How much
blood can a Black woman's heart pump until the body says it's had
enough doing, providing, suffering, saving, laboring, trending, and
tending, creating, owning, pushing,

supporting, empowering Black women don't know how to be one
thing   Who knew being a bad bitch could kill you
After all the strain death is what a job well done looks like

And I look over at my mother ready to come undone, but she don't
My mama hard and composed that way Like everything in this world
has beat on her to be

She sitting there like the doctor ain't told her nothing she ain't been
knowin' But for once, all her symptoms are affirmed without a
gaslight Today, she don't have to apologize for anything My mother
doesn't know how to unlearn something she's always been so good at
Our eyes meet   we're always changing places   sometimes I'm the
mother and she's the daughter In every lifetime, though,

I, too, am a horrible quitter

PUNK NOIR: THE BLACK WOMAN AS PROPHET

For Sister Rosetta Tharpe

So, me and all my badass walk into a bar, a club, a runway, or just any day,
and I got my grunge turned up:
got on all black everything, including my skin, but make no mistake—
I. Look. Good. In. Anything.
Cause all my amazing popped into Bantu, or bald, or mohawk—I'm so punk
rock, I got dreads for the dreaded, sista curls on swirl, but underneath it all,
my nature be natural
Star studded, spiked, and a boss chick for anybody who wanna try me
I'm just sayin', I'm so hardcore I get to be a Black woman
moshing through this life, swimming through all this pain
Even while restrained I reclaim
Hold me down long enough and I'll figure out how to turn these chains
into a crown
Busted it down and made sure it fit a Black woman aesthetic
Magic be my heritage with an unabashed identity
Call me the middle passage guru
DIY queen Yaaas hon-eey
No matter if it be fashion, music, art, or this body,
there ain't an idea you can have without me
Bush and tribe, the hive, the way we move and keep moving
Nonconforming
Proper and hood—it's a dichotomy, but you the only one confused
Made a way out of no way
Broke the glass   now the ceiling gone
You wanna act like a Black woman didn't do it,
haven't done it, and don't continue to school you
I made a subject out of myself
so even when they try to stop me, copy me, or erase me
I reboot a futuristic somebody and still stay the same:
touched and untouchable;
boxed and bothered;
vibrant and unsettled;
persistent, pierced, punk, and resisting

I got all this power I can't use
Made all these impressions, but somehow my bank account got reduced
My culture be endangered
Cause mainstream get to try on my attitude,
steal my face, and make all my Black woman trendy
without having to give a Black woman credit
But I showed up
like I been doin'
Allow me to reintroduce myself to the anti-establishment:
We the blueprint
a.k.a.
Black women been lit

POP QUIZ

So, I pose a question to Black men:
I ask, what do Black men hear when
Black women   say   PROTECT US?
What do Black men feel
they
have
done
to protect   Black women?
And for a long while,
      don't
none
of
'em

      say
      nuthin'
I grew up in a country where white people can
literally get away with anything
Where women work harder, got more degrees, and are valued less
Trust me, I know patience A Black woman waiting
is just another day ending in y
But I'm trying to learn something
Of course, I know what it's like to bear the weight of my choices,
to hope as a way to defy suffering for all that love and trouble brings
in defending what's mine or came from me my *niggah*
      I do it for *you* all the time
I interpret the silence as another example of the interpersonal
violence we experience
This is how we've come to know each other
Either I give you the answer or
I can't tell the truth about Black men without exposing myself
A growing soft spot for a lover I'm loyal to
Trauma-bonded and still know you'll claim to cherish and then kill
something as fragile and resilient and beautiful as me
But who needs a heart when there's subjugation?

Who listens to Black women without first
having them do their own emotional labor?
          Everything I do be magic
But I can't conjure a response from a *niggah*
that ain't having his own pissing contest
(trying to impress me with excuses)   and somehow that becomes
my fault, too

Let me be careful not to overgeneralize
I know *some* men think they doing it right, so they already offended,
and some men who don't wanna admit I'm talking
about them   be sensitive
Either way I don't think it's my fault when I can't tell
whether Black men's responses to Black women
and our protection is performative
You know Black men get to choose their conscious
Get to say what they should do as a way to pacify
and look past what they don't
Get to invite us to sit next to them
Included and mistreated, but don't expect us to say too much
Ball they fists up, get locked up, taken from us,
leave us to protect ourselves
You can know the definition of a word and still use it wrong
You can use *protection* in a sentence, describe it brilliantly,
but fail to make meaning of how you see me You can't be
pro-Black woman without being proactive in your actions
And I'm not saying I'm not aware of what this country has done
to our Black men,
but I also haven't read a Bible or walked into too many rooms where
a man's name or power wasn't mentioned or felt first and took up
space   He who finds a woman finds a good thing,
          so we should be grateful for these chains
Don't get me wrong, I've loved many men who can't help but think
          like a slaveholder
It's in the ways we've associated our worth to each other
The hand cannot say to the eye and the head cannot say to the feet, "I
don't need you"

Every day   I wake up,   a Black girl gets her wings,
and a man has the gall to ask if she was saved
Like she ain't had to cultivate safe spaces and act as her own savior
But go awf, King

One man said he learned to value Black women
once he saw his wife give birth,
and I thought of all the Black women who can't have
or don't want to or died during and still
am I to understand that Black men only value
what they can make use of?
Or is this the part of the narrative where
some Black men explain what they intended by what they've said

Another man said he gotta preference and she ain't Black
and then spouted something silly, saying
most Black girls don't even wanna get their hair wet or can't swim
And even after a niggah said something   I still held my mule
Gave him grace   let's say that's true   it ain't never stopped
me from trying to keep my head above water   or kept a
man from trying to drown me
You think I haven't learned how to love Black men
who watch from sidelines
mute my screams when they got too loud
Cause gotdamn! Black girls be loud and angry
Here I am again: only necessary when I'm not disposable
Still gotta be that b*tch
and walk these dogs to heaven

Another person suggested I talk louder
for the cis-Black men in the back
as if Black and gay or nonbinary don't benefit from
the image and mockery of Black women
He do you better than you do, sis!
Let us laugh at how strong
and brave
and tired

and witty
Black woman are, but aren't allowed to be
Let us be amazed at how
entitled people are to
the energy and time Black women give
And in every way I've had to endure without any assistance
(from you)
I'm still here
Rock and pillar
through plight And in all my methods of survival I still include
Black men
But some Black men only protect the Black women they know
or want something from
Let us pray you care for more than just (yo) mama
May you learn how to treat Black girls that are not born from curses
In every ear that couldn't hear me or haven't been paying attention,
the question means

        I need you

And then after I'm gone   know that I loved you anyway

II.

GIRLS HAVE TO BE RAISED. BOYS GET TO BE BABIED.

BIG BOOTY TIARA

My friend Tiara ask me if I can swim.

She got a body like a grown woman. We call her Big Booty cause she

gotta big booty. Big Booty Tiara, when she fancy. She wear the

tightest clothes. My cousin Desiree say that's how some women get

yeast infections. Panties too tight around they coochie. So, I stay

airing mine out. But not around boys, cause I know my scent

make they claws get thick.

Tiara short. You know ain't got no height and no titties, but

everybody see her booty when she walk, when she run, when she

coming around the mountain when she come a.k.a. the hallway. I ain't

jealous or nothing. I like my body fine, I guess. Mama say I'm

proportioned. I got just enough of everything in all the right places,

but all I need to be worried about is what's in them books. All the

boys know I'm smart—that's why don't none of em like me. Plus, I

got a mouth on me that remind them I hate they everything.

But Big Booty Tiara laugh at anything they say. I roll all of my eyes.

Girl, that nigga ain't even funny. I'ont even think he can read. He fah

damn sho ain't passing none of his classes. Nigga, minds well drop

out and study for his GED. She laugh anyway. Harder when they

touch her knee or slap that fat ass. Ain't nothing fat about me. Slim

thick what they call me. I ain't never want no nigga d*ck to get hard

off me.

One time we was at a party. Doing all the raunchy ass shaking, booty poppin', get low, hope yo mama don't walk through that doe kinda dancing. I'm pushing back real hard. Any nigga dancing wit me gotta hold tight to my waist. And right when I feel him losing his grip, I bruk it down real quick. Tell 'em, sit dat ass down, boi. You can't f*ck wit me. And all his boys, including my cousins, laugh wide as they can in his face. But Big Booty Tiara let 'em stay there and push up on it. Almost like they f*ckin or something. She said, Ebony, I felt so-and-so get excited. And I was like, Excited? F*ck that mean? She was like, You know, his weiner got hard or whateva. And I was like, Whaaaaaaa!? Girl, that's gross. And Big Booty Tiara said, That's how you know you doing it right. I'm tellin you, girl, you need to start dancing slow. And I was like, Hellll no, I'd rather dance by myself. Except for that one time when Joseph thought he was Usher or Ginuwine and he come slippin' and slidin' and quick footin' me. I watched 'em. I yawned. I'm like, okay my nigga, damn, you got happy feet. Then something real degrading came on, like Uncle Luke, and everybody got crazy cause that's the song we can all move fast to. But then the DJ mixed it out and Girl Gimme Dat P*ssy came on and everybody gotta slow up, but still use they ugly face for whoever they pushin' up on. You know, so everybody can tell you still gettin' it. And Joseph come pushin' all his goofy coordinated self on me. I let him stay. Put his hands around my waist. Find the rhythm in each other's beat. I bend over, but still keep a wind and small bounce about me. You know, syncopated and sh*t. And we grinding, you know, groovin'. And it ain't so bad. I'm having so much fun I start rollin' my back. And on my third dip, Joseph start biting his lips. He get low and make sure his bare hand rubbing my bare thigh. And I'm like, okay, I see why Tiara say it's fun when you go *slow*. But then Joseph crotch start rising and something hard start stickin' me. I kept dancing. But my eyes got bigger and bigger. But I don't want nobody to see him getting excited and think I'm feelin' this nigga.

So, I turn around. Cause maybe my booty where his brain is. So, now we rollin' and my chest keep rolling up against his chest. And his leg is in between my thighs. And Joseph keep closing his eyes while mine wide. He scoop me up and I'm so high off the ground I on't even think my feet can touch. And everybody started crowding around us, laughin' and tauntin'. Everybody got they hands up cheering, like we really doing something. So, I say, Put. Me. Down. And Joseph act like he ain't hear me say nothing. So, I wiggle and shake. He grabbing harder and harder. I'm trying to get my legs from around his waist, but Joseph is taller than me. I'm pushing all my weight from one side to the other, then Joseph lose his balance, drop us to the ground, and now he hovering over. I see Big Booty Tiara smiling while I'm reaching my hand out, mouthing, *Help me.*

Don't nobody do nothing. Not even my cousins. I think everybody thought I was enjoying it or somethin'. Joseph gruntin' and makin' wild d*ck thrust motions. The song finish and he hop up, adjust, and high five his friends. You know, like Joseph got a win cause Joseph was going in. I stand up, wipe the dirt from my butt, walk over to

Tiara with my hands up, sayin', Yo, fam, what the f*ck!? She smiling and laughing. A kee-kee nothing! Why y'all just let him hold me down, like I wasn't saying no or something? Tiara looked at me real plain without a smile and said, The boys ain't never gone want you if you don't let 'em think they can have you for just a little while. Now every time he see you, him and his friends gone wanna f*ck. And all you gotta do is be ready to give it up.

THIGHS (THE BLACK GIRL EDITION)

Royal tabletop of balance | Lap of grace | Ruler of smooth | Pillow of soft | shhhhh | com'er | lemme transform you. Holy holder of hard and heavy | head | head | and head. My thighs be mama-of-the-pat-pat | I put them babies to sleep. Bringer of thunder | no gaps | but crack wide enough to clap when she want to. Pretty brown | *in those jeans* | these thighs be too grown for their own good. Be balk and buck. Majesty of stank. Keeper of the milky wet | or | the red iron | or | kneeler to the men that pray | call *thighs* temptation. Savior to when these niggas need something to hold on to. Apron of conversation. The dog that jumped over the moon to see what my surfboard could do. *Graining on that wood* | Graining | *Graining on that wood.* My thighs still feel good in the morning after suffocating you all night. Issa revival | Either they conjuring the spirits or they is one. Whether it be shout | sweat | or release | all I know is | she | *rode that d like a soldier* | *She rode it like a soldier* | *She rode it like a calliope soldier.* Protector | Tree trunks | planted | Psalms and palms. Sky to where the stars fell | and death | left our sons to | rest. Big Mama of bend | Let us pray. Blessed be a | slim thick | medium thick | thick thick | Glory be these | thighs.

WHITE MEN SAY WEIRD THINGS TO ME

or do creepy sh*t they think I should be flattered by.
I've never dated a white man before. I'd like to think it's because I've
never wanted to stimulate my genetic trauma / or wanted that kind
of success to validate my accomplishments.

I don't think my ancestors would consider their rape raceplay and
call it sexy.

When I was in high school,
I remember my bus driver pulling the bus to the side of the road / near
the woods   some folks think the hood ain't got woods   but
some hoods do and I sat / stiff / rabbit and waiting / it is in the
silence where white men become the ones in every movie I've seen:
killers who still receive praises / Freddy Kruegers & Jasons. He
moves in slow motion to the back of the bus / he wants me to know
I'm seeing exactly what I think I'm seeing / and I wanna see how fast
I can run,   butIcantmove
so I try to disappear
          because how else are Black girls asked to use their magic?
But it's my heartbeat that gives me away // as he touches my hair //
my shoulder // my thigh // he says,
          "Every day after school, you leave the same way you came.
                    Pretty. Pretty. So pretty."
And that's it. That's all he wanted me to know. He said it three times /
so it must be true and traumatizing. Lets me off the bus
                    and I never skip track practice again.

In college,
a white boy from across the hall is sitting in my room one night
on my bed / in the dark / with his pants unzipped / says he mistook
my room for his.   If I move // will they call it manslaughter
or self-defense?

In Boston,
a white man tells me I look just like his mother, and I wonder if he
means his caregiver.
Another one in Houston
snaps a close-up and shows me /see /now I own you
            forever.
A white man in Wisconsin
flicks his cigarette at me and promises to find out what hotel I'm
staying in.

One time in Seattle,
I disappeared in a white man's blues.
I can't remember if his name was William / Robert / Richard / Gary /
Ted / or any other white man whose obsession with killing gets
romanticized for taking someone's breath away for collecting
            screams in jars   in basements in attics. / His voice was
gentle and conning / like I better be smart enough to keep my
freedom, / like I better know how to stay in my own body.
He asks if I want to go back to his place to eat some roasted pumpkin
seeds   That's some weird shit to say, huh?
Creepy, right?

White men taught me that being a predator is a compliment.
I should smile while walking / or running / or hiding. Shanequa /
Shantieya / Anna / Harmony / Caniya / a.k.a.
        no one turns over the Earth when a black girl goes missing.
It's only a matter of time before no one finds me / too.

I get so annoyed
when old men try to
holla at me.
Sir. Unless you plan
on making me a
beneficiary & dying
in the next few days
please leave me
alone.

SWAY

Dear Black girl,
you mispronounced wonder
You hand-me-down strange fruit
You bending-tree-splintered-and-spray rooted life
You stately-poor-mansion mouth with the stars falling out
You grip, grab, and growl
You hold on, stuck black
You surviving scorched temple
Sway.

You bob-head, battle-rap body, and graffiti tongue
causing cacophonies
You harmony and hip-hop booty
Legs
be standing
Be flyy
Be gathered razor smile and raging
fists
bulging in back pockets for the long walk home
Be ready
Be two-to-the-body and one-to-the-face
Be kicking, screaming
Be
calling all your pieces back
Be love
Be remembering how
you be Black woman
so
been know how
since mama taught you how to make a braid
and break bread with other Amazons
Gurl,
sway.

You balmy coil beauty making ruckus with your hair
You knotted brown black
You dark meat
You volcanic laugh

Say, I own myself
Say, I validate me and birth gods
Raised yo mama and yo mama's mama
ain't nothing but a mammy
taught you everything you know good
O, anyhow
gospel
O, hallelujah
Praise
Black girl,
sway.

Even when your bones hurt,
when they make wilt out of your name,
try and blow out your flame,
you be bigger
Show em you got that ether
Make em burn slow
You be inferno,
be progressive
Be fan, clap, and snap
This sh*t is magic—you'd have to be a Black girl to understand
Show em how it all got started,
how the bricks got laid
That this is what happens when the ink spills,
when your ancestors dance your worth awake

Dear Black girl,
sway.
Swoon.
WOOSH!

POCKETS

I want pockets
more than I want men
and politics, empty hands
and broken promises.
Women need pockets.
Not suffering or another
tomorrow that looks like
today.

I want pockets
to hold my own property.
I belong to me.
I get to decide.
And I say,
women need pockets
for survival and the
freedom to unleash every

b*tch and beast we've been
called and whatever else
that didn't belong to she/they
We need pockets.
Because privacy is not just
some luxury men
with dirt on their hands get
to keep.

How dare we be poems and
secrets we also get to hold onto.
Mouths and minds,
powerful, dangerous, deliberate,
and rebellious, women.
Give us pockets big enough to

turn parachute or fit into,
pull ourselves out of.
This woman's work be worth it.

I want pockets
more than I want patriarchy
and whatever else is ugly
and unserving.
I want pockets as tall as the
patience I've built.
As wide as the pain I've kept.
As long as the endurance I've

always had to have.
I want angry pockets,
messy pockets,
fun pockets,
slutty pockets,
exploding pockets,
or maybe just pockets
that will allow me to

escape from anything.

I want pockets so deep they
lose silence.

Or the state of mind that reinforces
the belief women are weak
and needy.
I want pockets that get to
mind or start they own business.
I want evaporative pockets that dissolve
tears, fears, lies, and garbage.
I want pockets for women born of

flames and a rage they couldn't blow out.
I wanna take my mouth out of my
pockets and let everything I say be fire,
so I can light yo ass up.

I choose violence.

I choose pockets that carry the heartbeat
of women who are fed up with not having
pockets. Here we are carrying hormones,
hatred, guns, depression, the Sun, and
open wounds. But, this time, I went inside
myself and returned as a machete, a hanger,
a chancla, and the Moon. Women need pockets
for protection.

I wanna release these hands
to dance and fight and fly
and write grief a love letter
saying it's time to let go now—
I gotta make room for me.

Give me pockets. Give me peace.

THE BLOOD

Many times I am asked if I have children.
And since I don't, I am then asked if I want one.

A woman without words.
I have so many words

to cover all my hurt feelings.
A womb with so many complex transitions.

They laugh when I respond with the name of a poem
I've spoken existence into and looks just like me.

Claiming a baby is not the same thing as a poem.
And a poem is not the same thing as a baby.

But neither are easy to make,
despite what you think.

Both are made from love or last minute.
Show me blood and brains what you really can do.

Conceiving at night.
Both are inside of me screaming.

Both can keep you up all night.
It's only by daybreak I know we've made it.

Splitting or bursting upon exit or entry
after a catalog of days have gone by.

Some push and come unexpectedly.
Some stop breathing.

Some cry their way through life,
because neither are easy to have or keep alive.

The blood, the poem.
My child had to come out one way or another.

For which you are never truly prepared for.
There is no manual on how to raise these poems.

I did the best I could
with what I had.

Babies require all of me.
Poems require all of me.

Both I have to care for.
Shield, defend, and stand behind.

Even if the baby is not happy.
Even if the poem is not a point of pride.

Both are a privilege and a chore.
I cannot say that motherhood or writing is always appealing.
I cannot say that children are always satisfying.

Poems are selfish,
always demanding attention,

tugging, pulling, asking, wanting.
The page, the pen, this world, its hunger.

I had to abandon myself for a poem I'd give anything to.
Have paid dearly in time for my children to love me back.

Because being a mother is not a luxury.
And that is what it means to be a writer, too.

Patiently waiting to be blessed.
Because a woman without is not a woman, I guess.

But I've pled to God before you were so rudely curious.
I plead and ask God to honor me with a baby

whom I can adorn and know what's the matter.
And God keeps giving me poems.

And I've come to learn wanting one and having one is not a solution,
but an expectation—if I'm going to call myself a writer.

And before I can hate you for not being me . . .
All these little Lexi's I get to nurture or neglect,

help them find their voice—
it's true,

I'm not always a good parent.

But you're not a writer,
so I wouldn't expect you to understand.

IT'S ALL MENTAL, isn't it?
The walls, the weight, and wait.
A closing in, a running round, a
already gone.
If everything is fine, why is my
mind trying to kill me?
Why does my heart keep lying,
pulling me along?

BODIED

My body requires too much while reminding
me that I am not enough.
My body finds mirrors and laughs at me,
all awkward and asymmetrical.
My body works out faithfully, but doesn't know
how to keep up with what
other bodies are supposed to look like.
My body should definitely pay closer attention
to what other bodies are

 supposed to look like.
Cause I really want one of those Teyana Taylor,
Tina Turner, Nicki, Badu,
Megan Thee Stallion hybrid bodies. But
all the body doctors I've talked to don't really see
my body's vision.
Why can't my body be one of those bodies
that looks good naked,

walking in slow motion, or doing nothing?
My body be so regular and unimpressive.
I think my body definitely looks better in clothing.
It's a Catch-22, though, cause I can't always find
clothes that look good on my body.
And still my body just wants to fit in, but poke out.

Be wanted by somebody that my body wants.
My body is in a complicated relationship with numbers.
My body gathers and collects guilt in large amounts.
My body doesn't get what it deserves; it gets what it can negotiate.
My body and its trauma responses,

counting, cutting, curves.
My body cries, hides, and gets sunk.
My body is slowly unraveling
into coping mechanisms after being triggered.
My body is lowkey exhausted.

My body and its lack of discipline always ready to give up.
My body can turn wounds to wisdom but somehow
still has poor body image.
Because what is a body, if not a shapeshifter?
My body is not a temple; it's a chandelier of strange fruit,
a museum of memories.

I don't always listen to my body.
And it's funny cause how can you say
body without also calling home?
This body I belong and come home to never leaves me.
My body wants approval first from me, then from everybody.
My body wants to be a wonder, but only with the lights off, so

you won't see my body and wonder.
My body wakes up early in the morning, only to disappoint me
by being a body without a filter or an airbrush.
Why can't my body be Barbie and Bad B*tch?
I wish my body was slim-thick.

And my body be so dramatic, making rolls in my stomach when I sit.
My body and its elaborate stretch marks, like spirit fingers,
and random weird body acne.
And I know everybody is different, but sometimes
my body really overdoes it by comparing itself to

others.
My body is lowkey passive aggressive.

Sometimes, I wish my body wasn't so annoying,
always wanting to be thought of.
When somebody tells me my body is beautiful,

my body has a hard time believing it.
One thing about my body: it's not for everybody.
But I wish my body was perfect.
My body is not perfect.
My body is perfectly imperfect and

I kinda love it.

COMING UNDONE

When someone takes their own life,
we do not say they killed themselves.
We do not talk about the anger
within or its visceral discomfort.
We do not say how much it hurts.
How confusing. How could you?
A body here and there's left.
A final decision seemingly so selfish.

We do not say how hard it is to resume
humanity and its brutality.
A windlass, some cannot balance.
A sinking, some cannot rise above it.
Sometimes the signs were hiding behind
what they pretended to cope with.

We say they were living, searching
for something they were unable to make fit.
They tried, but couldn't stick with it.
A sickness, unbearable emotional
pain they could no longer live with.
Continuing an intense, narrowed hopelessness.
They struggled to find the benefit.

If you're reading this and your heart is still swollen,
know your loved one's choices were not your fault,
and a solution was elusive. Talk about mental health,
the mind's running strong, and the coming undone.

GAY GOD

I.

If my son turned out gay, I would definitely disown him.
It would mess me up.
I wouldn't hate her, but I'd wonder where I went wrong as a parent.
I teach my kids it's not normal.
It's not natural.
You can't be born gay.
Gay is an abomination.
A danger to society.
Gay goes against my religion.
And then a gay person is killed by their religion.
How you know you gay?
Don't you know being gay will get you killed?
I don't like gay people; they just so . . . . gay.
Let's pray the gay away.
Let's get you converted.
I don't hate gay people; I just wouldn't want *my* kid to be gay.
And the child's first bully is their parents.
Ew, you gay?
Not in this house.
That sh*t gay!
This nigga gay!
Hell, nah, I ain't gay!
I used to have a friend that was gay.
I'll beat yo gay ass!
And then they got the gay beat out of them.
But not really.
And the post reads and the comments say.
And the gay kid couldn't take it anymore.
So, the gay kid killed themself.

II.

And the Bible says . . .
And the Bible says
our lives also include our sexuality.
Where you go, I will go, and where you stay, I will stay.
Your people will be my people, and your God, my God.[4]
And I thought God hates the gays,
but it's okay to quote the scripture of two lesbian women
as long as the vows are said in hetero.
Religious self-righteous people and their contradictions.
Since God created everything, so did The Creator
create Adam and Steve,
Eve and Lilith,
and allowed us to witness the intense relationship
between David and Jonathan.
But I guess you missed the story's meaning.
No man is perfect lest they be Jesus.
And everybody wanna be Jesus when they really
got Judas-like tendencies.
Too many have come to kill, steal, snitch, bitch, and destroy.
So . . . soooo incest and gang rape should be excused or kept secret,
but a boy kissing another boy is where you draw vigilance?
Interesting.
Every year during crawfish season, my family
has to make the decision
on how bad they wanna get into Heaven
and then show up to the cookout,
suckin' heads in mixed fabrics, tattoos, piercings, bad habits,
and multiple siblings with different last names.
Interesting.
Poverty and oppression are not the will of God,
but what is Church, if not a business preserved?
On Sundays, sometimes on the same day,

---

4. *The Bible*, Ruth 1:16-17

we praise and glorify a new idol
that's not God.
I swear to Beyoncé,
I cannot tell you how many times
a family member has told me they love me,
but do not agree with the life I live, because they've forgotten I know
their lives are not flawless.
Giving false interpretations to languages they know
not its translation,
but the collective expression of love appears over 300 times
because, above all things, God is love.
And since everyone is made in God's image,
how you gone tell God
that God
got the image wrong?
Gay people are not gay to bother you,
but, in fact,
are a testament to goodness and God's grace of everything that tried
to kill us,
and God still loves gay people anyway.
But you too busy doing the Devil's work.
I'm jus sayin',
if I'm going to Hell,
I'll see you there, too.

III.

To the gay people shut up in their bones
with flowers growing from their mouths and ears
somehow managing not to drown from being oversaturated
with loathing sounds spewed into spiraled thoughts of suicide,

(take a breath)

you do not have to hate yourself, even if someone else wants you to
die,
even if your parents do not choose to love you unconditionally.

You are not invisible.

They see you.

And your heart is so full. Your love is just right.

And so I say to you:

hold on and love you with all of your might.

Do not shrink or shy away; you are the gift that brought joy to the whole room.

Tell me what words you've been missing, so I can bloom you into healing

and remove all doubt.

Whether it be quietly kept or out loud.

I hope someone asks you if your significant other is good to you—

are they a good person?—

and that be the only worry.

Love is love.

Let this be a ring shout. Let this be a ring shout.

And the body remembers how to worship.

So, glory be to a God who looks just like you.

AFTER ROBERT FROST

I will be telling this with a sigh,[5]
as time flies by, I realize
more and more I
understand less and less
why "good" people do
f*ck sh*t.

---

5. Robert Frost's "The Road Not Taken"

PRAY TELL THEM

In this version of our Lord, God comes back as a dark skin fat Black woman who wears box braids, lace fronts, and melanin leave you shook. When I say she dark skin, I mean she can't pass and don't want to. I mean she walked into a room and everybody bowed instead of devoured that which is exotic. Cause in this version, dark skin actually means power, means royal & beloved, means lead role, lead singer, and more than just a few—so all the other dark skin big boned Black girls see themselves first. The original people. Call a God a God—I say it three times in the mirror, and I get to worship myself.

When I say fat, I mean she grew outside of your comfort zone or stereotype. Found a muthaf*cka to fan and feed her in the summer. And you gone get whatever body she givin'. I mean, if he die, then he die. And if he won't ___ her midday, then his ass gone freeze in the winter. I mean, shrinking is something she won't even consider. I mean her mouth be bigger than her stomach and she can do more with it than send yo food back. She be a meal and a snack. Cause in this version, God is not confident just because you noticed.

In this version of the holy trinity, Jesus is transgender. Black, woman, and savior. I mean, who else's gospel can turn colloquial? I mean, who else can identify as She or They and still be othered? Because who else can be praised, imitated, excluded, or under-represented. I mean, who gives a f*ck about respect as long as gay white men get to gentrify it?

She be beheaded, gunned down, and stoned. Everyone who wanted her dead called it a drop. But let's just say, she spun around so hard, so dramatic, soft, and slow, she became the Master of resurrecting on ballroom floors and moonlight waters.

Cause she can afford herself, but still not be free. I mean sticks and stones could break her bones, but a brick can start a riot. And there goes Jesus again, always turning turmoil into a celebration. Tested, but still holding fast to what's good. And Heaven is how high a queen sits.

We glow our hands up voguing Black queer culture into the Holy Spirit. How we see ourselves, well. Because only Black folks can behold a Holy Spirit who speaks truth to power and live without dwelling ahead of their time. I mean, who else gone shine? Be shedding, being, and keeping the light. God is everywhere. In and of everything. I mean, *Pray tell them*. God is love, right? So, you can go ahead and thank the Holy Spirit, that which is Black & queer, knowing and believing, *nothing moves without us*.

III.

I GREW & THEN I BROKE.

TANTRUMS OR HOW TO BE A POET IN SIX STEPS

Histrionic personality disorder is a mental health condition that affects the way a person thinks, perceives, and relates to others. A person with histrionic personality disorder seeks attention, talks dramatically with strong opinions, is easily influenced, has rapidly changing emotions, and thinks relationships are closer than they are. Treatment typically includes talk therapy.

1. If poetry was all the healing we needed, then God would've come back by now.

Good intentions do not erase harm // so // do // no // harm. Create boundaries. Those of us who give a lot often get little in return. But you still gotta wait your turn. Still gotta lift folks up, reach back, and put people on. Trust your gut—not everyone has the same heart as you. If you have to leave to be appreciated, then stay gone.

2. There will be people who are banking on you not knowing your worth. They will come dressed in community, but speak lackingly, baring disappointment, claiming to be non-confrontational and then do some f*ck sh*t. It's easier to write poems that are pretty than it is to have accountability. I'll tell you a story; it won't take long:

Once upon a time, I adored a woman who when she spoke it sounded like magic; she had a habit of making folks feel close // whole time she was just trying to stunt my growth or keep me from surpassing my master. There's something predatory and negligent in persuading fresh blood to write a poem and perform their trauma without making provisions or providing resources. But you can't fix what you don't know or what folks won't admit is broken.

I'll teach you a trick: If they say they love you, but you can't feel it, cause they don't show it or it feels manipulative, then that love ain't it. James Baldwin said, *People can cry much easier than they can change,* and I believe him, because I've seen it. Just as I've seen folks fake the Holy Ghost and call poetry Church. And I've never wanted to be a part of a congregation that helps me hide or parade my demons instead of healing them, but here we are. Poetry is not therapy, but a lot of us need it.

3. Okay. You wrote the poem, poet, but was it honest? Or is the poem only who you pretended to be? All poets are magicians hiding feelings in metaphors and hyperbole. God be in these poems, but I'm not perfect. My favorite illusion is living in a body that wants to survive with a mind that's trying to kill me. My greatest fear is dying unsatisfied. So, I'm trying to write myself into some place tender before I die. Poets stay trying to write letters to the universe to ask if we are enough; we wanna talk about our stuff and receive praise, but a lot of us still wanna remain the same. You want folks to get this work, but you don't really wanna do the work, poet. Poetry understands that grief is not linear, but wounds that go undealt with do not make you a profit. Sometimes you have to write the same poem twice. Once when you didn't know any better and the second time when you stopped holding the hurt somebody else gave you. When both hands are free, it's amazing what you can learn to do with them. I, too, had to remove myself from people who only valued what I could do for them by how much I was willing to endure. If you love yourself, the least you can do is be unavailable for bullsh*t.

4. Let your character carry more weight than titles do. Your poems are good, but do they resemble you? Along the way, you will meet so many versions of yourself, but which of you will you commit to? I'll tell you one thing about one thing: I've never gotten into it with someone I believed to be my friend over the color green. Some greedies confuse loyalty with money, move funny, and reveal who they truly are for the possibility of a possibility—break bread and then lie to you. They askin' for the blueprint to my win // someone has really got to teach us how to treat people. I'm callin' poets up, out, and in. You are // who you

are // what's mine is mine // and I've been hurt before, so I'm careful not to let too many in. There's a trapping that comes with celebritism and fame, but I promise I want peace more than I want attention. Finally financially stable, but I stay working on my mental – the heart is tough, but can still bruise easily. And I didn't die at 8 or 17 or 25 or 40. No bio can hold me; I do too much—just ask my pen. The cost of struggle is not transferable, necessary, or nobly noticed: I write the way I write as if the world I want is on its way back to me.

5. Your boundaries, your fee, your existence, and expectations are not suggestions. People and circumstances cannot stop blessings and abundance.

6. Your heart does not have to hurt for everything. Tell us: Is your poetry sunshine, is it air, does it exercise, dance, and breathe, drink water, pay attention to what is ingested and invested? Does the poet know when to rest, make love, and be woke? If you want poetry then you want God, which means you want laughter, freedom, and forgiveness. What would happen if you wrote a poem and lived a life that ended with you knowing you did what you came here to do? I should always remember to write about joy. And I always forget that I am my favorite. Each time I write, I am dedicated to teaching myself how to love. When I say I know my worth, what I mean is: have you ever seen an unf*ckwitable being? Therapy is a treatment plan that can teach the poet and the poem to stay present. But if you only write the poems to hear yourself talk, then you really won't learn the lesson.

A STRONGER LIE

What does not kill you makes you stronger[6] is a gotdamn lie!
There is a thing that happens all too well where we think we're overcomers,
as if the experience did not offer an entrance.
Resilient—
what good is it if I am still
stress(ed)?

There is a thing that happens all too well where we think we're overcomers and the poison did not get in.
Stress(ed) even when I'm begging.
What good is it if I'm still responding, defending, adapting?
Good grief to those who don't deserve what I do.
Left open holding, holding, holding a heavy I can't get rid of.

Stress(ed) even as I'm loving overlooked, unnoticed, untold.
Resilient left open holding, holding, holding a heavy I can't sleep—
my mind's a mess.
At least the clothes got washed, at least the house is kept; if I quit, will I starve.
Good grief, I did it while numbing; Imma die empty.
Because whoever said what doesn't kill you makes you stronger is a gotdamn lie.

---

6. Friedrich Nietzsche's *Twilight of the Idols*

IV.

YOU WILL BE GIVEN THE SAME TEST UNTIL YOU LEARN ITS LESSON.

HOW WE FORGET: COVID-19 FILES

After Loyce Gayo[7]

We forget that everyone is essential.
That there are no nonessential people.
That even when everything shuts down,
someone is still working to make sure we all don't give up.
I don't know how many frontlines make up the front,
but there's a whole lot of bodies trying not to give up.

We forget trauma is not always resilient.
We forgot the sound of sirens is the soundtrack to the hood.
And if you get out, this is still what it sounds like to be Black
in the hood.
Even before anyone ever mentioned racial disparities on the news.
Everything has been dying to live   here.
Some of us have to try harder than others.
Talam Acey says, *Maybe this is God's work.*[8]

I talk to God so much sometimes I have to go ahead and answer
myself.
We forgot to be patient. We forgot God is love.
We forget how to love.
We forgot to patiently love ourselves.
We forget we call people with mental illnesses crazy
if they talk to themselves.
We forget there is no one way to pray.

We forget some people only know one way to pray.
We forgot what prayer can do,
but know poems like the back of our hands.
We forget some people have only ever had their hands.
And a poem acted as a prayer to save us.

---

7. Loyce Gayo's "How We Forget"

8. Talam Acey's "G*D's Work (What if this is)"

We forgot how to be gentle and human.
We forget the loom of suffering does not mean survival.
Every day we forget how to do something,
but still manage to be believers.
We remember fight or flight.
But, somehow, we forget that some people freeze.
My friend Buddy says he's *not afraid to die,*
he just doesn't want it to hurt.[9]
But sometimes I don't know who I am without it.
I am only ever sure of what's constant.

One of my friends died during all of this.
In this moment in time.
One day she was here and the next day,
                    she wasn't.
There were only 10 people allowed at the burial service.
And I was one of the chosen. Standing. Socially freezing.

What I mean is
I've gotten good at being by myself;
I just don't wanna die alone.
We forget some people have only ever felt
                    alone.
We forgot we need each other.

We forget we are all essential.
That there are no nonessential people.

Distance does not always make the heart grow fonder.
We forgot about skin hunger.
We forgot some of us are aching to be touched.
It's been *x* days since I've gotten to see my partner's face.
We forget how time works.
We forgot time doesn't measure how much you miss someone.
All my body knows is she needs its person.

---

9. Buddy Wakefield's "Harmony Enemy"

We forget, in this lifetime,
there are people who have been waiting for what feels like
an entire lifetime.

We forgot some people have savings.
We forgot some people had to deplete their entire savings.
And still have rent, and school, and bellies,
and the bills come and don't stop coming.
We forgot some people still haven't caught up.
We know capitalism is King and elites have power.
But
we forget to be grateful.
We forget being grateful
and being satisfied
are not synonymous.
We forget some people have only ever known the struggle.
When people say it's hard out here, some of us are not making it up.
We know how to make a way. Real niggawds make do.
But if we're silent about our pain, they'll kill us and say we enjoyed it.[10]
So maybe
we forgot to stay ready for what is trying to kill us.

We forget some people aren't safe at home,
but still stay home, because they can't leave.
And I haven't forgotten about them.
I just remembered I don't know what more to do.

Sometimes I forget how good I got it.
Other times I forget to cry.
Mostly for me, crying has never solved anything.
I forget softness is not a weakness.
And crying doesn't have to cleanse everything.
I forgot I needed a break.
If not for this, I would've just kept going, despite myself.
I forget I have needs

---

10. Zora Neale Hurston's *Their Eyes Were Watching God*

And one of them is being mindful of taking care of me.
I forgot how to be present.
And being present and honest should not leave me stuck.
I forgot how to celebrate my own self,
even when no one can join me.
I need to know who I am when no one is watching.

Sometimes,
I think I wrote this poem because I'll never forget.
Other times
I know I wrote this because of how easily we forget.

PITY PARTY

The life of an artist is so fun and exhausting. On average, I perform about 50 to 80 shows per year nationally and internationally, which is a lot of traveling. I remember returning home from one of my trips and my partner of six years broke up with me. He walked into the living room the same time I was putting my bags down and was taking a seat. He sat across from me, and I could tell something was wrong. Without even looking me in the eyes, he said he wasn't happy anymore and I'm never home and whatever time I made for us wasn't enough. He was so matter of fact. It was almost as if I wasn't worth his time. Like I didn't deserve any more thought. And I don't know what that's like because I'm always thinking. I do so much for everyone, so to hear what I'm doing isn't enough hit different. One minute, you're sharing your life with someone and then all of a sudden you're not. I remember responding with, *I just want someone who will commit to not giving up on me.* I cried, I was really sad, but the thing about high functioning depression is you just have to keep going. In my mind, my life and all its balancing acts were no different than that of a teacher, a surgeon, or a stay-at-home parent. Right? Like, who doesn't have a to-do list and their goal isn't to get all the things on their to-do list done? So, on top of having my regularly scheduled program, I also have to move and find another place to stay.

Two months later, I have a miscarriage and I didn't tell anyone. Not my mom, not my best friend, my therapist, no one. I thought they would think it was my fault because I don't get enough rest, and I didn't need that. Sometimes my idea of resilience means to also suffer in silence. I tell myself it's not the best time for kids, I'm not sure if I can afford kids, and I don't even know if I want kids, anyway. Plus, how is this not a reminder of something telling me I'm not enough? I go to the urgent care and the physician recommends I rest and follow up with my OB/GYN. But I don't really have time for that. Sitting still makes me feel guilty, because there's always something to do and someone to prove wrong. Maybe a month or so after that, I start having car troubles. My heart sinks into my stomach because car stuff can be pretty stressful and I have a complicated relationship with money. Like, I know I have money, but I never know if I have enough. When my mom comes to pick me up from the repair shop, I get in the car and put my head in my hands. My stomach hurts, my eyes are twitching, and my head is swirling. At this point, I'm ready to cry big loud ugly tears, but before I can, my mom says, *Sometimes I wanna stop and have a pity party, too, but it never fixes anything when you still got stuff to do.*

And I just wanna have   a moment   to fall   apart.

But I don't. And I tell myself, even though life can be taxing, unprecedented amounts of stress should not keep me from succeeding. So, I sit up, take a deep breath, stuff my tears back down my throat, and continue my life on autopilot. A few years later, I find myself Googling HOW TO KNOW IF YOU'RE HAVING A NERVOUS BREAKDOWN, because I'm holding back tears, the headaches are getting worse and lasting longer, and my blood pressure reads 142 over 96. By medical definition, I'm currently at risk of having a stroke. The physician this time tells me, *Even if resilience comes as a result of adversity, stretching yourself to capacity is not a healthy or sustainable measurement of self-worth.* The repeated trauma and stress have real effects on my physical, emotional, and mental health. Resilience isn't always about how much suffering you can overcome. Sometimes it's how much grace and patience and time and love you stop to actually extend
             to yourself. I don't know if I've learned the lesson, but now I don't just consider what is the worst thing that can happen. I also ask myself: *What is the best thing that can happen if I just give myself more than a moment to rest?* Because the saying *what does not kill you makes you stronger* is a lie.

THE ART OF QUILTING

My grandmother made quilts.
Wielding. Needle to the point. She'd work her fingers small and
tender to the bone.
I only know women who love like this.
Twist and tie. Sew and thread. Loc and keep. Scrap pile. Nothing gets
thrown out.
She made use of everything. Had mercy. I'm still learning what it
means to let go of the things I no longer need. My grandmother took
her time cutting edges, loving straight, or whatever it means to be
careful and do the right thing. A square that went days without being
touched—you can sound tough and be riddled with anxiety. You can
have a smile so big, but happiness never reaches your eyes. Tethering
jokes out of disappointment; who do you think you're fooling?
As above, so below.
A daily fret. What of all the ageless heirlooms and scrape of weight
waiting to turn grace. My grandmother is a snake doctor, patch-
working imperfections. A pattern-master—sometimes we stay longer
than we should. A lover packed with baggage, still a nimble being.
My grandmother, balanced in putting signs together to understand
things. I used to think I had to hold onto relationships at all cost. But
what of my own padded craft & comfort? Shadowy these hands. Cast
spells.
My ancestors whispered for me to *save something for myself.*
I still have so much to unlearn. But my grandmother has never tried
to be perfect for people who have no idea of how to make something
perfect. Just a handmade shield, frayed, heavy, and pulsating light.
A rare quality cut from a different cloth—and everybody know it,
'cause everyone can feel it.
My grandmother,
once spread over fabric, stayed-stitching fine bits and pieces, she
loved people well—even when they gave her too much. Blood, sweat,
and clutter, for all the time it took—A bumpy smooth life she built
soft   persevering her energy
I'm still learning, it seams.

V.

THE UNIVERSE WILL NOT MAKE A LIAR OUT OF YOU.

BATTLE CRY

Be real *Black* for me.

Come into being the

Blackest you

      you've ever seen

Be so Black, you purple

A royal hue

Let the blues blue

Let the hips swing

Let the laugh loud

Stick your tongue out

Body of Afrobeats

be thunder twerker—wonderfully made

You are quite the beauty.

Be real *Black* for me.

Shimmer a glimmer of all this   be rooted

Stretch joy across your face

Show all your teeth

Hurting once seen

Now surviving survival mode

Listen to Black Moses:

If you hear the dogs, keep going . . .

Don't ever stop. Keep going.

Don't forget you made it

It's in your blood   Born

Your ancestor's wildest dreams.

O New day, O Black hole Sun

And melanated movement

Squeezing Bending Ache without breaking

Speak in your mother's tongue

Be alien   not from   here

Been life'ing this life for a while now

Been tired and sad Been down before

O Triumphant, O Galactic giant And

                              Living legends

Filled with fear,

          get free with me Freedom,

Run into this

chanting *Akoben*

Calling our peoples names   *Bring some; get more*

Show *Egun*,

You remember *the bounty of life*

Be real *Black* for me   a never scared

Sacred beings in our regalia   Shine on.

MENTAL HEALTH_BARZ

I'm an artist.
Which also means
I'm a creator because I create things.
A storyteller since I have stories to tell.
A visionary because I write about where I've been.
       These poems act as self-help.
I'm a healer, not always for myself.
But one time, a kid told me he almost killed himself,
but he heard one of my poems and decided to keep living.
And from that day forward, I was convinced   today
is a good day to keep someone alive.
People ask me how I did it or how they should do it.
And I'm not sure if they're asking me about the kid or themselves.
But what I've come to learn is   no one can tell when I'm not
doing well   but me.
I get to travel across the country and do poems. For a living. Like,
that's my job. And out of 50 states, I've performed in 48 of them. I
read an article one time that said only 20% of people in the US are
doing what they love (or whatever sad statistic it was). And I'm like,
My God, ain't damned nothing in me   I'm doing exactly what I've
always wanted to do, so I must be

blessed
Must be exemplifying all this miracle.
I am stressed and winning. I look at and update my curriculum vitae
daily and I be like,
Damn, I'm impressed I even knew how to say that word, and
ain't nobody wished nothing bad on me but me. Like everything I
ever wanted I manifested.
At the end of each meditation, I ask the universe to help me be
undeniably enough.
And people be mad happy when I show up.
One time, I performed for 200,000 people and I didn't throw up!
It was so cool and exhausting. Did you know I can touch what feels

like a million people's energy and help them feel seen,
but go back to my hotel room feeling so fulfilled, yet
lonely?
Yeah, it's amazing!

Another time,
I thought I was going to marry this guy
I had been with for, like, six years out of my life.
But he said he hated my lifestyle, even though this is my life's work,
because my work means I'm "never home,"
but every time I came back, he was gone.
As in emotionally unavailable.
Mentally abusive.
I have extreme PTSD from that unhealthy relationship.
But someone asked me to do that one poem
about that one time
when he was

                                      mine.
May you find a lover that helps you to love yourself.
May you find a lover that doesn't require you to give more to them
than you have to give to yourself.
                        Did I mention I paid off my student loans
with POETRY?!?
                                            Can't.
Nobody. Tell. Me. I'm. Not. The. Sh*t.
but myself.
I get so sad sometimes I think I'm losing my mind.
And I must be,
because I enrolled in graduate school this past May.   I guess I
returned to my oppressor.
I am whoever I think I am.   But I wish being a
good person paid more.

I heard it's the wounds folks can't see that hurt the most.
But I've seen sunsets that look like somewhere tomorrow
                     my heart is on fire.

So, I'm chasing the day. At night. I don't sleep. I grind.
I been in my prime, like, nine times.
I got so much love. I give. And keep giving.
I have so much advice that is actually opinions
or maybe they're just hard facts I haven't hardly learned yet.
Did you know there are people who ask me how I'm doing
by also commenting on my weight?
And here I am, some foolish somebody
who didn't actually hate the way they look today.
But you right girl, must be the depression.
But I'm the kind of giant that's been through
what I've been through and you can still depend on.
I gave the last of what I had.
And you ain't never known a black woman who ain't did that.
My friends call me when they're down and out or just
                    in need.
And what good is a God that can't speak life into somebody?

Check on your strong friends.   Don't believe us.   I promise
we're just pretending.

Have you ever tried to tell people you're not okay and they're like,

You're doing good.
And you're like,
But I'm not.
And they're like,
You got this!
And you're like,
But I don't!
And they're like,
Keep going.
And you're like,

Okay. Thanks.

You're right. I could do this with my eyes closed.

I'm so overwhelmed, one time I was drowning and screaming,
but everybody thought I was swimming and smiling.
I died in that dream. Then I woke up on an airplane flying to a
different country to do   poetry.
And I thought,
My God, ain't damned nothing in me.
I'm doing exactly what I've always wanted to do.
           I'm so blessed. I'm so blessed. I'm so blessed—
my life is crazy.   My heart is racing.   I'm
probably dehydrated.
Traveling does some awful things to the body.
But the one thing I know about being successful is you have to love
what you're doing.
           Can't nobody steal my joy. Can't nobody steal my joy.
Not even myself.
Somebody said if your path is more difficult, it's because your calling
is higher.
So, I say I be hero and legend.
Nobody built like me; I designed myself.
But every time I climb, my community get cosigned.
Divinity defined.
Cheers to the most high.
I just pray I leave something good

behind.

"Mind of goddess.
Heart of a street nigga."

IN MEMORY OF SACHA "THE SAUCE" ANTOINETTE

LUMINARIES

God, Orishas, ancestors, & my mama—thank you for being everything for everything. To my sister, I never knew I'd have to live this many days without you in my life. I miss you. For my family & close friends, I'm grateful & glad I don't have to wonder, guess, or beg. To my community & my tribe, *one day when the war is won, it'll be ours.* It is with endless gratitude and indebted thanks to Angela Rye, Ayokunle Falomo, Roya Marsh, Natasha T. Miller, Rudy Francisco, & Michael P. Whalen. Doggon Krigga, you the future and the fortune. Thank you, Button Poetry, for affirming my boldness. To the reader, thank you for celebrating *BloodFresh* and being believers in me. To the writing time-traveler (self), I'm so proud of you.

Credits
Photographer: Harris! | Instagram: HarrisShootz
Hair: Sherrah Chester | Instagram: MatchMyHands
Shirt: Diamonds Anjell | Instagram: Diamondsanjell
Crown: Mariola | Instagram: Mariolacraftings

ABOUT THE AUTHOR

Ebony Stewart (also know as the Gully Princess) is a Black woman born into the hands of complicated Black women with long memories that speak with passion, and cuss. She is an award-winning international touring spoken-word artist born and raised and still resides in Texas. She reps the H proudly and is one of Baytown's finest. Ebony has a BA in English & Communication Studies and is currently obtaining her Master's in Clinical Social Work Therapy where she hopes to work with and provide affordable therapy to artists. Her work aims to validate the human experience and provide a layered perspective of mental wellness by recalling through poetry, storytelling, and reflection. Ebony's work has been used within secondary and institutions of higher education. She has been a guest lecturer and performer at a number of colleges and universities across the U.S. Ebony has shared stages and worked alongside varied artists such as the late Amiri Baraka, Marsha Ambrosius, Jeremih, Angela Rye, and UK Drag Queen, Vinegar Strokes. Outside of being a mentor, friend, and auntie to many in the poetry community, Ebony has also done voice-over work for RedWing, is an award-winning playwright, and developed a curriculum from her *Home.Girl.Hood.* manuscript. Ebony Stewart is a poet, a spoken-word artist, a writer, performer, author, and observer of the life she's living. Her previous books of poetry, *The Queen's Glory & The Pussy's Box*, *Love Letters to Balled Fists*, and *Home.Girl.Hood*, are available at her website, EBPoetry.com. She is always appreciative of genuine support.

OTHER BOOKS BY BUTTON POETRY

If you enjoyed this book, please consider checking out some of our others, below. Readers like you allow us to keep broadcasting and publishing. Thank you!

Neil Hilborn, *Our Numbered Days*
Hanif Abdurraqib, *The Crown Ain't Worth Much*
Sabrina Benaim, *Depression & Other Magic Tricks*
Rudy Francisco, *Helium*
Rachel Wiley, *Nothing Is Okay*
Neil Hilborn, *The Future*
Phil Kaye, *Date & Time*
Andrea Gibson, *Lord of the Butterflies*
Blythe Baird, *If My Body Could Speak*
Desireé Dallagiacomo, *SINK*
Dave Harris, *Patricide*
Michael Lee, *The Only Worlds We Know*
Raych Jackson, *Even the Saints Audition*
Brenna Twohy, *Swallowtail*
Porsha Olayiwola, *i shimmer sometimes, too*
Jared Singer, *Forgive Yourself These Tiny Acts of Self-Destruction*
Adam Falkner, *The Willies*
George Abraham, *Birthright*
Omar Holmon, *We Were All Someone Else Yesterday*
Rachel Wiley, *Fat Girl Finishing School*
Bianca Phipps, *crown noble*
Rudy Francisco, *I'll Fly Away*
Natasha T. Miller, *Butcher*
Kevin Kantor, *Please Come Off-Book*
Ollie Schminkey, *Dead Dad Jokes*
Reagan Myers, *Afterwards*
L.E. Bowman, *What I Learned From the Trees*
Patrick Roche, *A Socially Acceptable Breakdown*
Andrea Gibson, *You Better Be Lightning*
Rachel Wiley, *Revenge Body*

Available at buttonpoetry.com/shop and more!

FORTHCOMING BOOKS BY BUTTON POETRY

Kyle 'Guante' Tran Myhre, *Not a lot of Reasons to Sing, but Enough*
Steven Willis, *A Peculiar People*
Topaz Winters, *So, Stranger*
Siaara Freeman, *Urbanshee*
Junious 'Jay' Ward, *Composition*
Darius Simpson, *Never Catch Me*
Robert Lynn, *How to Maintain Eye Contact*